The impossible Physics

Where Artificial intelligence and human innovation conquer the impossible

Dantee Obazee

Copyright 2023© **Dantee Obazee**

All rights reserved. This book is copyright and no part of it may be reproduced, distributed, or transmitted in any form or by any means, including photocopying, recording, or other electronic or mechanical methods, without the prior written permission of the publisher, except in the case of brief quotations embodied in critical reviews and certain other non-commercial uses permitted by copyright law.

Printed in the United States of America Copyright 2023 © **Dantee Obazee**

Contents

Introduction 1
Chapter 1: Impossible Physics 2
Chapter 2: Artificial intelligence 7
Chapter 3: AI's Opportunities and Challenges 16
Chapter 4: Recent Developments in Impossible Physics 25
Chapter 5: Possibilities for Impossible Physics Applications .34
Conclusion 38

Introduction

What if I told you there was a location where the seemingly unattainable became a reality? a location where human ingenuity and machine intelligence meet, leading to previously unthinkable feats?

Welcome to The Impossible Physics universe. Everything is possible here. We can accomplish the unthinkable by combining cutting-edge technology and unadulterated human inventiveness. We are continually pushing the edges of what is feasible, from defying the rules of physics to traversing the bounds of space and time.

What then is Impossible Physics? In this environment, anything is conceivable. A place where the unthinkable is made possible and dreams come true.

Chapter 1: Impossible Physics

The seeming existence of impossibly hard physics in the natural world has long perplexed scientists. But precisely what are they?

Simply put, occurrences that defy accepted principles of physics are known as impossible physics. Things that shouldn't be feasible exist in front of us despite the fact that they shouldn't be. The double-slit experiment and quantum mechanics are two of the most well-known examples.

Many of these occurrences have been explained by theories like quantum mechanics, but others of them are still a mystery to science. They make us reevaluate how we perceive the world and the universe in general, which is why we find them to be so fascinating.

The study of phenomena that defy the known rules of nature is known as impossible physics. It involves the exploration of the unusual and unknown, and it frequently contradicts what we believe to be true about the cosmos.

Time travel, travel at the speed of light, and parallel universes are some of the most well-known results of impossible physics.

Scientists are continuously trying to figure out how each of these hypotheses works because they each offer up a whole new world of potential outcomes. It's a fascinating field that is always changing. Who knows what we could learn about next?

Definitely it is a field of interest with several prospects. The addition of AI to this subject makes it the more interesting.

How Impossible Physics Work

According to the Impossible Physics theory, there may be an alternative world that is quite similar to our own while also having some significant deviations. The physical laws that we take for granted are changed in this parallel reality. For instance, in our cosmos, gravity causes objects to be drawn toward the earth's center.

However, in the alternative reality, gravity would cause items to be drawn away from the ground.

The ramifications of this theory for physics and astronomy are intriguing. One benefit is that it might enable us to understand some of the peculiar spacecraft phenomena. Second, it might enable us to solve some of the puzzles surrounding black holes. Last but not least, it might aid in the creation of fresh and enhanced methods for producing energy.

Consequences of the Impossible Physics

Everything is feasible with artificial intelligence and human ingenuity, as demonstrated by the laws of physics that seem unattainable. Therefore, technological advances like teleportation, time travel, and even molecular manipulation are within the reach of our society. We might witness significant developments in computing technology, medical research, and space exploration if the two factors are combined.

With limitless potential comes a greater responsibility to use this power for good. The possibilities are endless. We should be aware of any ethical concerns this ground-breaking technology can raise, such as possible data misuse or privacy concerns.

For now, it's critical to keep in mind that, despite the fact that concepts from science fiction might appear to be unattainable at the moment, they are actually attainable if we continue to collaborate and use our imaginations to propel us ahead. We can achieve the impossible physics by embracing new technology and working together as scientists, engineers, and entrepreneurs!

People would have thought you were insane if you had told them that physicists had found a technique to travel faster than the speed of light a few decades ago. But it really did turn out like that! We'll examine some of the most recent developments in the study of impossible physics in this post.

The principles of physics have so far been disregarded in a number of ways by scientists. For instance, they have developed particles that can produce miniaturized black holes and move faster than the speed of light. Even time travel may be possible, according to some experts!

Even though many of these discoveries are still being investigated, they could completely alter how we perceive the cosmos. To understand more about these amazing developments in improbable physics, keep reading!

Chapter 2: Artificial intelligence

Imagine being able to use artificial intelligence to increase your creativity and productivity. In a variety of areas, AI has already begun to support human innovation, and this tendency will only grow.

Although artificial intelligence has been around for a while, actual applications have only lately started to be made. And AI is responsible for innovations like self-driving cars and automated customer service representatives.

The study of artificial intelligence, also known as AI, is a branch of computer science and engineering that aims to build intelligent machines, or computers, that are capable of carrying out activities that typically require human intelligence, such comprehending language and object recognition.

AI, or artificial intelligence, is a rapidly expanding area of computer science that deals with the development of intelligent agents, or autonomous reasoning, learning, and acting systems. In other words, the goal of AI is to create autonomous machines.

Although it might sound like something from a science fiction film, this is truly happening. Everything from voice recognition to cancer diagnosis to self-driving cars uses AI. And there are countless opportunities.

Examining the Relationship between Humanity, Physics, and Artificial Intelligence

Although they might not seem to go together, physics and artificial intelligence actually have a lot in common.

Artificial intelligence is the study of intelligence, or the capacity to learn and comprehend challenging tasks. Physics is the study of the natural world. When you combine these two disciplines, you gain a completely new understanding of both: you can see how physics can be utilized to build more intelligent AI and how AI can be used to mimic and even improve natural processes.

The prospect of creating sentient life forms has always attracted humanity, and as AI develops further, this interest will only intensify. What then lies ahead for physics, AI, and humanity? Join us as we investigate this intriguing subject.

People have always been interested in physics because it is the basis of the cosmos. It is the study of the underlying ideas that underpin all of nature. The development of our technology is also based on it.

There are no limits to what is conceivable, we are discovering more and more as we investigate and solve the secrets of the cosmos. The marriage of human ingenuity and computer intelligence has allowed us to advance our understanding of physics to unprecedented heights.

Together, we are pushing the frontiers of what was previously thought to be impossible and exploring new worlds. We are already making progress toward goals that were formerly considered unattainable. Because of the cooperation between humans and artificial intelligence, the future is promising.

How is AI Shaped by Physics?

What comes to mind when you think of AI? You're probably envisioning a scenario like that in 2001: A Space Odyssey or the Terminator movies, in which computers become conscious of themselves and vow to obliterate humans. However, AI is actually much more complicated than that.

Making devices that can learn and change on their own is at the heart of artificial intelligence. You must comprehend the fundamental tenets of physics in order to accomplish it. This is due to the fact that physics is the basis of everything in the natural world, including life.

We wouldn't be able to build computers that can realistically "learn" and evolve if we didn't understand physics. In reality, physicists have contributed their understanding of quantum mechanics and Chaos theory to the discipline, leading to some of the most significant advances in AI.

Making Use of Physics to Perform the Impossible

There is no denying that human ingenuity and artificial intelligence are doing things that were previously unthinkable. But what's even more astonishing is how they're collaborating to accomplish even bigger objectives.

Consider the work being done in the discipline of physics. It has long been regarded as one of the most difficult and complicated disciplines out there. But the toughest physics obstacles are being met and overcome because of the combined strength of AI and human intelligence.

This is but one illustration of how AI and human invention might combine to accomplish the unachievable. When these two forces interact, the possibilities are endless, and we've only begun to scratch the surface.

Actionable Examples of AI and Physics

Have you ever heard of the laws of physics that defy logic? It's where human ingenuity and artificial intelligence (AI) come together to remove obstacles that we previously believed were insurmountable. Here are some examples of how AI and physics interact:

1. By examining patterns and forms, AI can detect items in a video or image considerably more quickly than humans can do so manually.

2. Even in complex physics-based systems where conventional methods have failed, AI can be used to forecast outcomes and suggest courses of action.

3. In robotics, artificial intelligence (AI) can assist robots in navigating difficult terrain and modifying their movements in response to incoming data, making them more effective, precise, and secure to use.

4. AI may be used to find patterns in data sets, which enables physicists to make discoveries that were previously impossible.

5. AI can even aid in quantum computing since it can quickly assess potential states of a quantum system that would otherwise take scientists far longer to calculate by hand.

As you can see, when it comes to impossible physics, there are a lot of opportunities for increased efficiency and productivity, especially when combined with the strength of artificial intelligence.

How AI is used in several fields

You undoubtedly want to know how AI is being used in various fields.

AI is being employed in a number of different ways to support human invention. AI is used, for instance, in business to manage inventory and forecast customer behavior. Businesses may better manage their resources and produce goods that customers will actually desire to purchase.

AI is being utilized in the medical industry to identify illnesses and assist surgeons in their surgical planning. AI can potentially be utilized to speed up a patient's recovery following surgery.

AI is being utilized in the field of education to help teachers analyze student progress and to build tailored learning programs for kids. AI may be utilized to develop adaptive tutoring programs that improve student learning.

Chapter 3: AI's Opportunities and Challenges

Both amazing potential and serious challenges are presented by AI. On the one hand, it might hold the solution to many of today's most serious issues, like the environment and world hunger. On the other hand, it prompts a variety of moral and ethical issues that we must address if we want to ensure that AI is applied properly.

Although the task is difficult, it is not insurmountable. To achieve this, we must make sure that everyone working on AI development—from governmental organizations to small businesses and huge corporations—is held responsible for their part in developing ethical AI solutions. Additionally, we must make sure that laws are in place to safeguard citizens from potential harm brought on by its wrongful usage.

Last but not least, we need to work together to develop a shared vision for how AI may be utilized to improve our society without jeopardizing privacy or general wellbeing. To come to a solution that pleases everyone concerned, it will be necessary for all stakeholders to work together and contribute their individual perspectives.

What Potential Benefits Might AI Have for Humanity?

Artificial intelligence is proven to be a great ally for humans when it comes to the seemingly impossible. Consider the most current advances in quantum computing.

Humans are now able to solve challenges that were previously thought to be insurmountable because to the development of AI. AI is enhancing human invention and assisting us in finding solutions to challenges that we would never have been able to find on our own because to its capacity to analyze enormous volumes of data and spot patterns.

This is but one illustration of how AI is improving our lives. The possibilities are unlimited as we improve this technology. AI has so far been used to develop better cities, discover new energy sources, and treat diseases. Thanks to the potential of artificial intelligence, the future appears to be more promising than ever.

Fortunately, artificial intelligence has a lot to offer the human race. A few of these are:

- AI can assist us in finding solutions to issues that we couldn't find on our own. For instance, it can assist us in figuring up fresh and creative solutions to challenging mathematical puzzles or new sources of energy.
- AI can aid us in making wiser decisions. For instance, it can assist us in sorting through vast amounts of data to discover trends and insights that we otherwise wouldn't be able to perceive.
- AI can facilitate quicker decision-making. For instance, it can speed up information processing or let us to perform computations that would take a lot of time for a human to perform.
- AI can assist us with task automation. For instance, technology can assist us with regular

chores that would take a long time for a human to complete, such as writing code.

What Are the Humanity Risks of AI?

There is no denying the close relationship between physics, artificial intelligence, and humanity. However, any significant innovation carries some risk. AI has raised a variety of moral conundrums, including concerns about sentient robots taking over mankind in the future and employment losses brought on by automation and autonomous weapons.

We struggle to foresee the outcomes of technological advancements in AI, both favorable and unfavorable. Others have expressed concerns about an even wider gap between the "haves" and the "have-nots" as these technologies become more common. Some experts have predicted that AI-driven technologies will soon bring about a utopia—a world where abundance is the norm and poverty is eradicated.

It's crucial to think about how we might minimize the risks while maximizing the advantages as we continue to study the interface between AI, physics, and humanity.

What Can We Do to Manage and Harness AI's Power?

What makes the study of AI so fascinating is the possibility to combine human insight and creativity with machine learning techniques. AI can assist us in making decisions and finding solutions to issues that we might not have been able to find on our own. However, it can also speed up the process.

For instance, you might utilize AI to produce a vast array of potential answers and narrow them down based on their efficacy or efficiency rather than spending hours or days attempting to come up with a complex solution on your own. This would offer you a far better foundation from which to innovate and solve problems going forward, allowing you to concentrate your efforts on tasks that machines might not be able to perform as well as people.

The possibility for quicker invention cycles is also offered by this fusion of human and machine expertise. We can iterate more quickly and examine more ideas at once than we could otherwise by combining the abilities of humans and technology. This greatly lowers the risk involved with experimentation while simultaneously increasing the likelihood of finding effective solutions more quickly.

Ultimately, there are both significant risks and tremendous opportunities at the nexus of Artificial Intelligence, Physics, and Humanity. But how can we use AI's capabilities for the good of humanity as a whole?

First and foremost, it's crucial to guarantee data security and accuracy. Given how valuable data is, it is crucial to make sure that only reliable information is incorporated into AI models. This will make it less likely that incorrect inferences will result in erroneous decisions or manipulations.

Second, it can be useful to look at cutting-edge controls for AI technologies. Regulations ought to be written to assist innovation while also guaranteeing that privacy and safety standards are upheld.

Finally, it's important to educate ourselves about artificial intelligence. It's critical to have a thorough grasp of how this technology operates and what potential effects it might have on society in the future in order to make informed decisions about the regulations governing its use.

Getting Ready for AI disadvantage on Human Society in the Future?

The potential of artificial intelligence is enormous and will only increase.

In a variety of areas, AI is already enhancing human invention. For instance, it is assisting us in hastening the process of product design and development. Additionally, it makes it simpler for us to recognize and assess consumer demands. Additionally, AI is assisting us in producing better content and choosing more efficient marketing strategies.

For companies ready to adopt AI, the future is looking promising. AI will undoubtedly play a significant role in fostering innovation and growth in the years to come thanks to its capacity to enhance human potential.

The future of humanity is significantly impacted by the development of AI technology. We need to consider how AI might change our lives and how to be ready for its effects.

One action we can do is to keep studying and learning about how physics, artificial intelligence, and mankind interact. This entails becoming more knowledgeable about the ethical ramifications of AI for security, privacy, and safety as well as how AI may be able to aid in energy conservation and climate change mitigation.

At the same time, it's crucial to acknowledge that AI has the potential to significantly enhance many facets of our lives. AI, for instance, can be utilized to create smarter transportation systems that lower emissions and traffic jams. It can be used to develop personalized healthcare solutions that continuously track patient health. Additionally, it can be utilized in education to deliver individualized learning opportunities catered to every student's requirements and talents.

We can make sure that society is ready for the potential effects of developments in AI technology by investigating this interesting nexus of artificial intelligence, physics, and humanity.

Chapter 4: Recent Developments in Impossible Physics

In recent years, the field of impossible physics has made some amazing strides, and as a result, our concept of the cosmos has undergone a significant change.

For instance, researchers have recently shown that it is indeed feasible to travel faster than the speed of light and that it is not a physical restriction. This might have profound effects on how we perceive space and time, as well as spur the creation of novel scientific and technological advancements that will enable us to explore the cosmos in ways we never imagined.

Parallel worlds have been discovered to exist, which is a significant advancement in the subject of impractical physics. Parallel worlds have long been thought of as the stuff of science fiction, but recent developments in quantum mechanics have proven that they might actually exist. This could result in ground-breaking new findings regarding the nature of reality itself and has profound consequences for how we perceive the cosmos and our role within it.

Quantum Computing and the Physics of the Impossible

Many of the limits we currently face with classical computers may soon be eliminated by quantum computing. These restrictions result from the basic makeup of the digital components that make up traditional systems. However, in a quantum system, the laws are different.

Quantum bits (qubits) can exist in several states at once and be both a one and a zero at the same time. This creates a completely new method of computing and information storage. We would be able to tackle issues that are today intractable and store more data in a smaller amount of space with the help of quantum computing.

The possible uses of quantum computing may seem like something from a science fiction film, but they are actual and fascinating. Researchers are already exploring applications for this novel technology. So who knows what incredible things we will be able to accomplish in the future with the impossibly physics?

Teleportation and the Impossible Physics

Have you ever fantasized of transporting your friends and yourself to a new area instantly? What if you could make that happen by using the improbable laws of physics? Even though this type of teleportation may seem like something out of science fiction, it might actually be feasible.

This is because teleportation would be made possible by the principles of the impossible physics, which would allow us to change the nature of space-time and move across it (or at least our energy). Even though it might not be a typical form of transportation, it could be utilized in an emergency to quickly move injured individuals from one place to another.

Additionally, as these particles travel through space faster than the speed of light, scientists anticipate that they will be able to more effectively investigate far-off stars and galaxies than ever before. The ability to send data and communications faster than light speed would have an impact on communication as well.

Quantum mechanics' most recent developments

When you think you have a solid grasp on your surroundings, scientists appear and utterly upend your assumptions.

A subfield of physics known as quantum mechanics studies the extremely microscopic universe of atomic and subatomic particles. It was once thought to be purely theoretical with little use in the real world. But because to some extremely creative research, quantum mechanics has recently made significant advancements.

The field of quantum teleportation has produced some of the most astounding discoveries. Without any actual particle movement, this is how quantum information is transferred from one location to another. Up until now, researchers have been able to transport quantum data over distances of up to 100 kilometers. The ability to teleport matter and energy will improve as our knowledge of quantum mechanics advances. And this is just the beginning.

The Multiverse Theory: An Examination

There may be an endless number of universes, each with its own set of physical laws, according to some physicists. The multiverse theory is the name for this hypothesis.

This notion is still being researched, and methods to test it are being developed. Some people think that interdimensional travel might be conceivable. Others believe that by hunting for gravitational wave evidence, it may be able to find proof of other universes.

There is currently no proof that there are other universes. The multiverse theory is a fascinating concept, though, and scientists will undoubtedly continue to investigate it in the years to come.

Potential for Time Travel

Recent developments in the field of Impossible Physics may have made you aware of the potential for time travel. Time travel, to put it simply, is generally regulated time travel, such as going back in time or even into the future.

Theoretically, this would enable someone to travel back in time, relive certain moments or events from their past, and even change their past if they so desired. Naturally, there are still many limitations on how this can be feasible, such as the results of any paradoxes that would result from altering the past.

But don't let it discourage you—scientists are still investigating the feasibility of time travel and have thus far discovered some fascinating findings!

Integrating quantum mechanics and general relativity

The two most influential theories in physics, general relativity and quantum mechanics, may be familiar to you, but you may not be aware that they are truly incompatible. Yes, they don't fit together, and this is what has prevented us from coming up with a single, comprehensive theory of quantum gravity.

These two potent hypotheses can now be combined thanks to recent developments in the realm of impossible physics. Theorists have advanced the hypothesis that gravity is not a fundamental force but rather an emergent behavior resulting from underlying microscopic interactions between atoms by combining concepts from thermodynamics and information theory. This idea gives us optimism that one day we may be able to combine general relativity and quantum mechanics into a single coherent theory.

Consequences for How We Understand the Universe

For our knowledge of the universe, recent developments in the subject of impossible physics are extremely important. This has created new avenues for investigation and the testing of current theories in order to better comprehend how and why matter acts the way it does.

The possibility for us to be able to handle objects more adeptly than we previously thought conceivable is one of the most fascinating breakthroughs. For instance, it is conceivable to produce objects with the ability to exist in two locations at once using quantum mechanical forces; in other words, an object that exists in two points of space-time simultaneously.

This indicates that we may theoretically build materials and structures with unfathomable qualities by modifying matter at the atomic level, such as being both solid and elastic at the same time or having the ability to bend time itself! It is difficult to even decide what applications the consequences of this discovery might have on our daily lives.

Chapter 5: Possibilities for Impossible Physics Applications

The unfeasible physics has broad and far-reaching effects. We've just just started to scratch the surface of what's conceivable so far.

Consider potential applications as an illustration. It would fundamentally alter the way we live if we were able to use the power of the impossible physics. In only a few seconds, we could reach distant galaxies. We could produce an endless supply of energy. We could eradicate poverty and hunger worldwide.

There are countless options. And that's only the start. Who knows what we'll find out as we continue to investigate the consequences of the improbable physics?

Harnessing the Impossible Physics: Challenges

The difficult thing now is that, despite the Impossible Physics having a theoretical foundation, it is not necessarily practical to implement. In actuality, there are certain significant obstacles that must be overcome before you can even start to become a reality.

To begin with, it takes a lot of energy to access and manage the Impossible Physics. This implies that we would require a technique of massively storing and transferring energy, which has eluded scientists thus far. Additionally, creating the technology to harness this energy is a difficult task in and of itself and might call for cutting-edge materials that don't even exist now.

Finally, the Impossible Physics are unpredictable by their own nature, which means that any attempt to use them may have unanticipated results. Before we can begin using this potential new source of energy, it is crucial to think about how these implications might affect already-existing laws, regulations, and societies as a whole.

The Impossible Physics' Future

What does this improbable physics have in store for us in the future? We can't be sure, but what we do know is that it might lead to a whole new world of opportunities.

As you can see, physics' practical limits are being pushed by human ingenuity and artificial intelligence. Together, they are taking on some of the most challenging issues and bringing about a more optimistic future.

It might, for starters, fundamentally alter how we see and deal with physical items. We could be able to influence objects in ways that have never been possible before by altering the known laws of physics. This might result in some incredible scientific and technological discoveries and advancements.

Beyond merely manipulating physical items, this technology has the potential to completely alter how we relate to time, space, and energy. We might even be able to travel at the speed of light or discover whole other universes and realities.

What do these developments therefore portend for the future? First and foremost, AI will probably be used to design more effective systems, such those that conserve energy in homes and cars. AI may potentially be utilized to create novel, less expensive, and more resilient materials and chemicals. AI may also aid in our understanding of the cosmos as a whole, facilitating more physics breakthroughs.

The consequences of these improbable physics are enormous, but it will take years to determine how they will affect our reality.

At the same time, technological development and further research into the region of impossibly hard physics will be driven by human invention. Thanks to innovations produced by remarkable minds that don't settle for the current quo, we'll keep exploring fields like quantum computing, dark matter research, and interstellar flight.

Conclusion

In conclusion, it's incredible to see how human ingenuity and artificial intelligence can combine to overcome the seemingly insurmountable. In the field of artificial intelligence, we are moving ever-closer to an era in which anything is conceivable. We're excited to see what the future holds and know it will be as spectacular as the seemingly impossible physics we've discussed in this post.

All things considered, it is clear that AI is enhancing human ingenuity in a variety of ways. Even if there may be some worries about how artificial intelligence may affect human jobs in the future, it is obvious that AI is already having a positive impact and will do so in the future.

What does this mean for humanity, then?

We're entering a new era where artificial intelligence will play a significant role in our daily lives. It is our responsibility to ensure that everyone, not just a chosen few, benefits from the usage of this technology. We must make sure that AI is used to address existing issues rather than causing new ones.

Although it will be difficult, we are up for the challenge. To ensure that the future is bright for all of humanity, let's work together.

www.ingramcontent.com/pod-product-compliance
Lightning Source LLC
Chambersburg PA
CBHW070321220526
45465CB00013B/2050